HAL•LEONARD

Classical PLAY-ALONG™

Volume 16

Luigi BOCCHERINI
(1743-1805)
(arr. Friedrich Grütznmacher, 1832-1903)

Cello Concerto in B-flat Major, G 482

The Hal Leonard Classical Play-Along™ series allows you to work through great classical works systematically and at any tempo with accompaniment.

Tracks 2-4 on the CD demonstrate the concert version of each movement. After tuning your instrument to Track 1 you can begin practicing the piece. Using the Amazing Slow-Downer technology included on the CD, you can adjust the recording to any tempo you like without altering the pitch. (Note that when using Amazing Slow-Downer, the CD will stop after each track instead of playing continuously.) The full cadenzas are played only in the concert version.

- Track No. ☐ – tuning notes
- Track numbers in circles ◯ – concert version
- Track numbers in diamonds ◆ – play-al...

CONCERT VERSION

Rustam Komachkov, Cello

Russian Philharmonic Orchestra Moscow

Konstantin Krimets, Conductor

T0080097

ISBN 978-1-4234-6255-2

HAL•LEONARD®
CORPORATION

7777 W. BLUEMOUND RD. P.O. BOX 13819 MILWAUKEE, WI 53213

In Australia Contact:
Hal Leonard Australia Pty. Ltd.
4 Lentara Court
Cheltenham, Victoria, 3192 Australia
Email: ausadmin@halleonard.com.au

Visit Hal Leonard Online at
www.halleonard.com

CONCERTO NO. 9

for Cello in B flat Major, G 482

L. Boccherini (1743 - 1805)
Arrangement: F. Grutzmacher

I ②

3

5

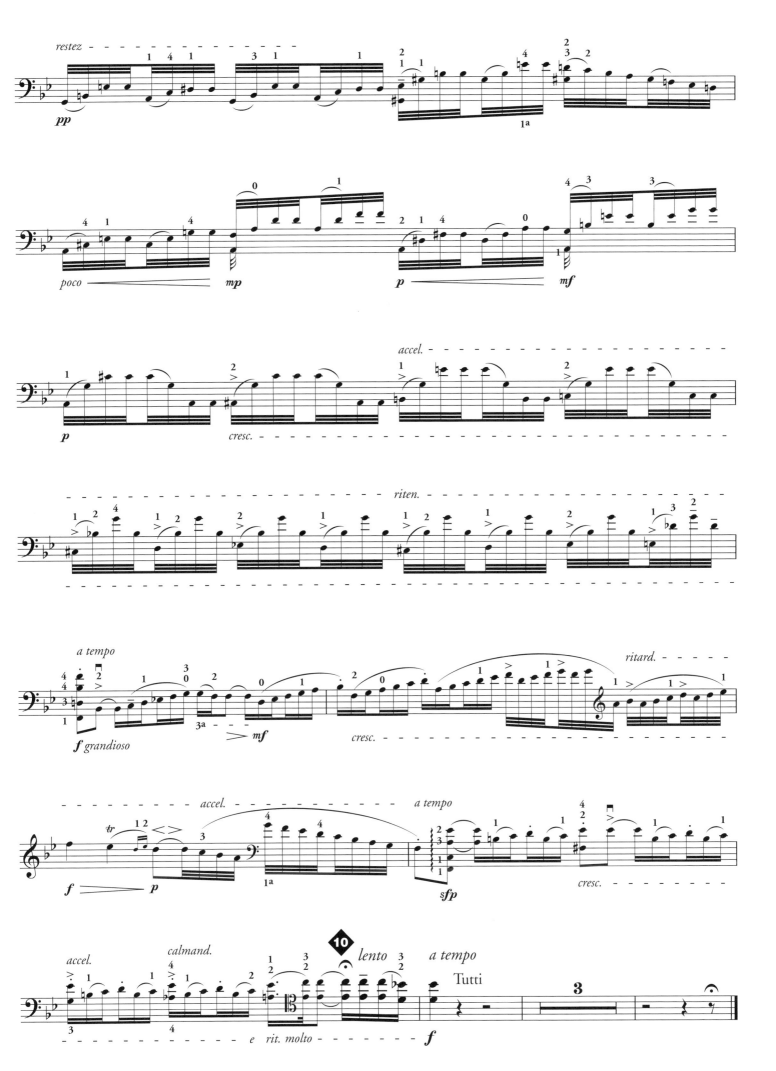

7

III - Rondo ④

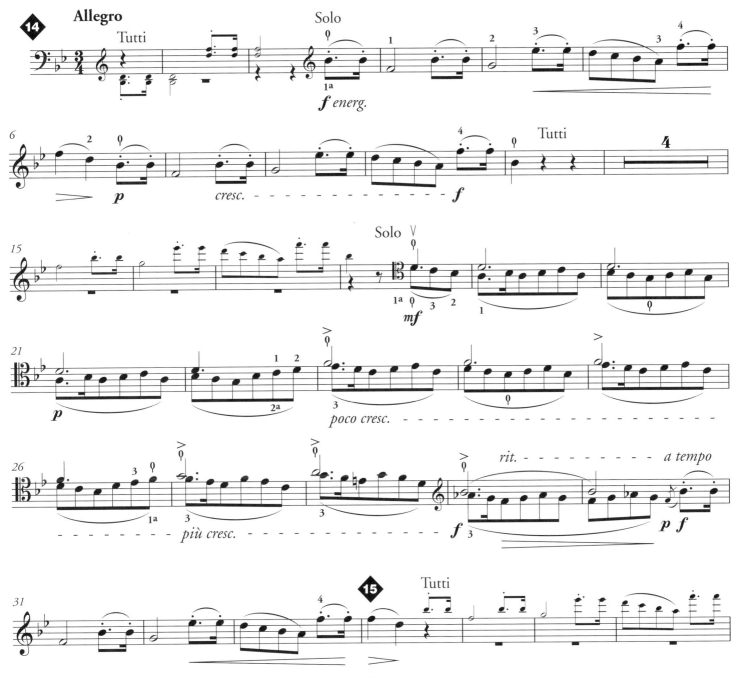